Feng Shui

Improve your wealth, home & office, and eliminate clutter for harmony, balance and prosperity

Table of Contents

Copyright.. 1
The Basics of Feng Shui 3
    The Benefits of Feng Shui 3
    The Origins of Feng Shui 4
    How Feng Shui Works.................................... 5
Yin Yang and the 5 Elements................................. 9
Feng Shui and the Environment.......................... 15
    Surrounding Establishments and Objects. 20
    Elevation... 24
    Shape of lots... 25
The House/Building and Interiors 26
    House/Building Shape 26
    House Size and Dimensions 27
General Feng Shui Guidelines.............................. 36
Conclusion... 37
Bonus Content 38

Copyright

1

The Basics of Feng Shui

Feng Shui is a 6,000 year old Chinese practice that deals with the manipulation of a universal force called "chi" for people's benefit. The words feng and shui literally mean "wind water", both of which direct chi in the environment. According to Feng Shui law, wind scatters chi while water collects it. The name signifies the practice's purpose of controlling chi energy to achieve certain purposes.

The Benefits of Feng Shui

The goal of Feng Shui is to direct the flow of "chi" in a place to let good energy in and remove bad energy. When this is achieved, the following benefits come as a result:

- Comfortable living
- Better health
- Improved vitality
- Peaceful sleep
- Enhanced protection
- Career and business success
- Financial prosperity
- Harmonious relationships

- Psychological well-being
- Increased creativity
- Clearer mind
- Support from people
- Fame and respect
- Overall good luck

These are only some of the advantages of practicing Feng Shui. This book will teach you how to manipulate chi to achieve your specific goals.

The Origins of Feng Shui

The ancient Chinese used Feng Shui in carefully planning out where they put up structures. Conditions in ancient China were severe: constant flooding, strong mountain winds, and other natural disasters forced the Chinese to study how nature runs its course. Feng Shui scholars were funded by the Chinese royalty to help improve their life conditions. Their knowledge was kept away from the ordinary people back then, and practitioners were forbidden to share what they know outside of the royal court.

Despite this prohibition, there were rebellious Feng Shui masters, such as Yang Yunsang, who helped poor people through Feng Shui. Over the years, the tight grip over Feng Shui information was relinquished and people of all walks of life got to learn about it as well.

How Feng Shui Works

Feng Shui works through interconnections between matter and energy.

Interconnectedness

Feng Shui operates on the principle that everything is interconnected. Although Feng Shui predates Taoism, it has adopted the Taoist belief that says, "All things are connected and unified in the Tao (the Universe's creative principle)." Other cultures, such the Greeks and the Indians, also believe in a unifying principle although they call it by different names and they have their own explanations for it. This is not limited to cultural concepts, though. Philosophers ponder about oneness and non-duality throughout the ages.

Scientists have proposed theories that seem to confirm mystics' and philosophers' beliefs. To name a few examples, Albert Einstein's theory of relativity describes mass and energy to be one and the same, while quantum physics theories point to linkages of all matter and energy at the subatomic level. These prove that the Feng Shui concept of interrelatedness is not limited to Chinese culture but it is observed and thought about by many.

Feng Shui deals with the interaction of three things:

- Heaven – heavenly chi, time, celestial bodies (sun, moon, stars), and the weather
- Humanity – human chi, life-force, bio-electricity
- Earth –earth chi, geography, man-made structures, locations, magnetic fields

Feng Shui methods aim to control these forces to create positive effects in a person's life. They work on the idea that a thing exudes chi that interacts with chi from other things, and the interplay of these forces has effects on people and their life experiences.

Chi / Qi

Chi (also spelled as Qi) is said to be the vital force that runs through all things – time, space, matter (living and non-living), and energy. Fritjof Capra, physicist and author of the Tao of Physics, defines the "field of chi" as the underlying essence of all objects and the carrier of mutual interactions among them. Chi has counterparts in other beliefs – prana (Hindus), spiritus (Catholics), ruah (Hebrews), pneuma (Greeks), tane (Hawaiians), Ki (Japanese), orgone (Wilhelm Reich), animal magnetism (Franz Mesmer), and so on.

It is normally invisible, although some people say that Kirlian photography captures this invisible energy. It can be sensed through other means, such as through the intuition and emotions. Its effects can be observed through the qualities of the objects in there, the events taking place, and the inhabitants' experiences and life situations. Although the existence of chi is not yet proven by traditional science, it hasn't stopped people from believing in chi and working with it.

Feng Shui handles chi by evaluating how chi functions in a place and rearranging / placing / removing objects in order to produce a good energetic flow in that location.

Types of Chi

There are two main types of chi according to Feng Shui: sheng chi and sha chi. Poison arrow chi is a variant of sha chi.

- **Sheng Chi**

   Sheng chi is beneficial chi. It nurtures you and opens up wonderful opportunities for you. You can sense the presence of sheng chi if something appeals to you. This kind of chi arises from objects, situations, or interactions with other people. For example: pleasant sceneries, sounds of nature, comfortable couches, your favorite meal, good vibes, etc.

- **Sha Chi**

  Sha chi is harmful chi. It is responsible for bad things in life such as diseases, accidents, disharmony, failures, and bad luck. Anything that repels you or makes you ill harbors this energy. For example: rotting food, garbage, unwashed clothes, air pollution, bickering, physical violence, distrust, depression, etc.

- **Poison Arrow Chi**

This is negative chi that injures you energetically – and since energy and your physical body are connected, along with other aspects of your life, you might get ill or unlucky as a result. This radiates from pointed corners, aligned doorways, straight paths towards you, and other things that are sharply directed towards you.

One easy way to practice Feng Shui is to bring in objects and experiences that promote your well-being and eliminate those that are disruptive. Allowing the energy to flow naturally requires you to avoid or at least minimize poison arrow chi. Watch out for straight lines and sharp edges in your environment. Energy flows more freely in wavy lines, and the smooth movement is essential for the energetic balance within you and around you. If you can't remove the sources of poison arrow chi, find remedies for it. This will be discussed later.

Yin Yang and the 5 Elements

Yin and Yang express the duality of the Universe. Generally, Yin is the passive principle while Yang is the active principle. They have other correlations, with Yang representing strength or superiority and Yin embodying weakness or inferiority. The list below is not a comprehensive one; Yin and Yang associations include contrasting seasons, emotions, activities, directions, mode of thinking, colors, shapes, subjects, and more.

Yin	Yang
Passive	Active
Female	Male
Dark	Light
Cold	Hot
Wet	Dry
Night	Day
Stillness	Motion
Descending	Rising
Soft	Hard
Even numbers	Odd numbers
Right side	Left side
Bottom	Top
Inward	Outward
Death	Life
Bad	Good
Nurturing	Aggressive
Angles	Round
Blue, Green	Yellow, Red

The Yin Yang symbol (Tai-chi) signifies the unity and complementarity of the opposites. The circle stands for the unified whole where the forces dwell and move about. The Yang symbol is depicted by the rising white shape with a black dot or eye, which means that it contains a seed of Yin within itself. The Yin symbol is drawn as the descending black shape with a white eye. It likewise contains a seed of Yang in it. This expresses the notion that everything has the potential to change into its opposite, and things are constantly changing.

Feng Shui remedies deal with Yin and Yang. A place becomes harmonious when its ying and yang components are balanced, or when the dominant energies are compatible with the activities in the place. Familiarize yourself with each so you'll have an idea of what it means when you're instructed to add more yin energy, for example.

The Five Elements

The 5 elements of Feng Shui stand for the five forms of chi:

- Fire: chi that radiates outwards
- Earth: chi that compacts
- Metal: chi that contracts or withdraws
- Water: chi that descends
- Wood: chi that rises or grows

These 5 elements are involved in 3 kinds of cycles:

Creative Cycle

Fire -> Earth -> Metal -> Water -> Wood -> Fire
This process involves one element giving birth to another. To explain, fire leaves earthy ashes behind, earth produces metal within it, metal condenses liquid, water makes wood grow, and dry wood bursts into flames.

Destructive Cycle

Fire -> Metal -> Wood -> Earth -> water
In the destructive cycle, each element controls and destroys another. Fire melts away metal, metal chops wood, growing trees crack the earth, earth dams up water, and water extinguishes flames.

Weakening Cycle

Fire -> Wood -> Water -> Metal -> Earth -> Fire
A weakening element negates the effects of a controlling element upon a weaker element. By referring to the creative cycle, you will find a weakening element in the middle of 2 clashing elements (elements next to each other in the destructive cycle like fire and wood). This serves as the balancing factor between the two. The arrangement of the elements in the weakening cycle is the same as that of the creative cycle, but with the order reversed. Thus, fire tames wood by feeding upon it and producing earth – thus, weakening wood's damaging effects on earth.

Wood tames water by absorbing it and fueling fire, relinquishing water's powers over fire. Water hinders metal's destruction upon wood by nourishing it and corroding metal. Metal counteracts earth's blocking force upon water by moving earth away (through digging with a shovel, for example) and generating more water. And finally, earth mitigates fire's destruction upon metal by smothering flames and building metal.

Using the Elements and Cycles for Feng Shui

Like Yin and Yang, the five elements have correspondences assigned to them. This is also a simple list – associations extend to directions, body organs, senses, emotions, actions, virtues, etc.

Elemental Correspondences

Elements	Weather		Times	Materials	Colors	Shapes
Fire	Hot	Noon, Summer, Adulthood, Growth		Anything that produces heat or light, Shiny fabrics	Red, Pink, Purple	Triangle, Sharp angles, Pointed
Earth	Wet	Afternoon, Late Summer, Midlife, Maturity		Anything from the earth (ex. clay, stones, sand, concrete, tiles, porcelain, crystals)	Brown, Tan, Yellow	Square, Boxy, Flat
Metal	Dry	Sunset, Autumn, Old age, Harvest		Metallic objects, Wires, Glass, Shiny surfaces, Wind chimes	White, Gold, Silver	Circle, Rounded shapes, Curves, Domes
Water	Cold	Midnight, Winter, Death, Rest		Flowing water, Aquariums, Glass, Humidifier	Blue, Black	Wavy, Irregularly shaped
Wood	Windy	Early Morning, Spring, Birth, Youth		Living plants, Natural fibers, Flowers, Fruits, Vegetables	Green,	Tall, Rectangle, Columnar, Oblong

Using the chart given above, observe the place and determine what elements are present there. If there are conflicting elements (see Destructive Cycle), refer to the Weakening Cycle to know what element to use to bring back harmony.

For example: your room has blue walls and red

curtains. This is a destructive combination because the colors represent water and fire. Since fire is the stronger of the two, read the weakening cycle to find out what tames fire: earth. You may add earth colors and materials to your room to promote good Feng Shui without having to remove your curtains or repaint your walls. Take note that other things aside from color (like the ages of the occupants and the feel of the place) also create elemental chi.

If the dominant elements have a creative relationship to each other, such as water and wood, you don't need to put in an extra element to balance them.

Feng Shui and the Environment

Feng Shui assigns deities, seasons, colors, elements, energies, and features to the four directions (North, South, East, and West). You may either use the compass directions or the four sides of the property. Both methods work.

The Four Directions of Feng Shui

North/Back
Black Turtle
Winter
Black
Yin Chi
Water
Highest structures
For protection and support
of the back

West/Right
White Tiger
Autumn
White
Metal
Yin Chi
Has a raised structure lower
than Dragon side and may
have flowing water
To protect and support sides

House
Building
Main structure

East/Left
Azure Dragon
Spring
Green
Wood
Yang Chi
Has a raised structure higher
than Tiger side To protect
and support sides

South/Front
Crimson Bird
Summer
Red
Yang Chi
Lowest features
To give a clear view of front

15

Follow these basic guidelines to attain good Feng Shui:

- A high landform or structure is positioned at the back of the property (it could be a mountain, tree, building, or high wall)
- The front is a wide and clear space
- The left side (when looking out from the inside of the property) should be lower than the right side, or have a waterway
- The right side (from the inside) should be higher than the left side, or have a road

The property must not be built in the lowest area of the land to prevent floods and chi stagnation (because water and chi pool to the lowest levels)

It's believed that chi emanates from mountains and high structures, thus an area with a tall structure behind it can receive the chi. Tall structures also protect the property's chi from being scattered by the wind. A place with a protected back translates into protection from vulnerability for the area and the occupants. Since the back of the house represents the next generation, it symbolizes that the children will surpass their parents. However, make sure that the high object does not obstruct sunlight – it is needed to bring positive energy and dispel negative forces.

A wide and unobstructed area at the front of the

property allows the occupants to have broad perspectives and unhindered undertakings.

The Chinese believe that the tiger is destructive. The property's left side or tiger side is recommended to have a waterway to calm the tiger and prevent it from harming the residents. However, water at the dragon side may also work if there is none on the Tiger side. Avoid having a road or a driveway on the tiger side – a busy street can activate it and cause misfortune.

In contrast, the dragon is seen to be beneficial. The dragon side should ideally be higher than the Tiger side to bring in helpful friends. If the land is flat, the entrance of the house and the garage can be placed in the Dragon side to let chi flow in.

Roads/Rivers

Road activity and flowing water stirs up energy, and it tends to stay in motion unless another force or structure impedes it. The kind of road/s or waterway that surrounds the home or building affects the chi that goes into it. As mentioned in the beginning, straight roads harbor poison arrow chi, or fast-moving energy that damages the energy field of anything that obstructs its way.

Practically speaking, a path headed straight to your house can cause an accident when a car's breaks malfunction. Aside from that, sharply curving roads can likewise cause vehicles to careen off course and into your lot. Like vehicles, chi also follows the street and cause energetic disruptions when the road is straight or steeply curved. Thus, when choosing a location, consider the roads and streams that surround it. The road descriptions are also applicable to rivers.

Straight roads. A road in front of the house is okay for as long as it's not a busy street or freeway. An active street produces noise and air pollution, which are forms of sha chi. A dead-end street stopping at your house is very unfortunate because the momentum of the chi will break the energy in your home.

T and Y junctions. A T junction is similar to a dead-end but with roads at right angles to it. A Y junction has two pathways angling away from the straight road. They have two kinds of sha: stabbing sha (caused by the incoming vehicles) and depleting sha (caused by the departing vehicles). This combination causes disasters and depletion of resources. Do not position your property in front of the straight path of a T or Y junction.

Parallel roads. If your lot is in the middle of parallel streets, it will receive conflicting streams of energy and it will feel ungrounded.

Corner lots. A corner lot has a road in front and at one side. Ideally, the house should have protection at both left and right sides. If one is missing, the energy may become imbalanced. If the road is at the back of the house and there is no stable structure separating the residence from the street, the energy of the place may become vulnerable to sha.

Sharp bend. When the property is near the edge of a sharply curving road, it will receive energy that's similar to poison arrow chi. The energy from the road will also scatter the good chi that has accumulated in the property. Additionally, vehicles may accidentally drive into the lot, since it's difficult to maneuver tight bends.

Narrow U-shape. A house nestled within a tight U-shaped road may suffer from chi congestion that's caused by the piling up of energy from three of its sides.

Gently curving roads. This kind of road is good when the house is loosely embraced within the bend. The curve allows energy to move smoothly and distribute evenly into the property.

To summarize, the best locations for property are those with a peaceful road/river in front of it and those within gently curved roads/rivers.

Surrounding Establishments and Objects

Nearby buildings and things will exert their influence upon the property. Avoid the following when selecting your location:

- **Electrical towers, telecommunication towers, and power stations**. These produce electromagnetic frequencies that produce negative effects on the physical and psychological health of people. Both Feng Shui and science agree that it's unwise to stay near these structures.

- **Schools.** Youthful, active energy from a school can reach your home and cause sleeplessness and exhaustion.

- **Industrial zones.** These produce noise and smoke, which affects people negatively. The activities in these areas may cause restlessness.

- **Police and fire station.** These two places are associated with negative events such as crimes, accidents, and destruction. These may have an impact on the psychological well being of people, and the energies may attract similar events into the house. The loud sirens of fire trucks and police mobiles often cause annoyances.

- **Airport.** Living near an airport means dealing with loud engine noises. The hustle and bustle of people produces disruptive chi, causing people to become uneasy.

- **Railroads.** The sound of blaring trains can be stressful for those who live nearby. Also, the chi that the trains push along may become too strong and turn into poison arrow chi. Railroads can be dangerous especially for children.

- **Hospital.** Although joyful events happen in hospitals (such as the birth of children and the healing of illnesses, for example), negative events also occur there (illness, death, pain). Hospitals are havens for all kinds of powerful emotions and traumatic memories. These energies can radiate outwards and contaminate the atmosphere in a home.

- **Cemetery or Funeral Parlor.** The energies of grief and death can make people sick or emotionally unstable. They may also trigger hallucinations and ghost sightings.

- **Church or Temple.** These spiritual places may seem like good neighbors but it's not recommended in Feng Shui. They deal with Yin energy, which is incompatible with everyday life. Like hospitals, they contain a variety of strong emotions that may adversely affect residents.

- **Narrowly spaced high-rise buildings.** If a house is in the middle of two towering buildings that are close together, or if it's directly facing them, it will be the target of sha chi that slides down along the two buildings' walls. This may severely harm the energy field in the house and cause fires and accidents. Other than that, the towers may dominate over the house and cause inferiority complexes among the people in it.

- **Tall building among low structures.** The building is exposed to winds that scatter the chi, so it won't be able to accumulate auspicious energies. Without anything taller than it, the building won't be supported. It will stick out like a sore thumb and its chi will be inconsistent with the environment.

- **Old and broken-down house among new homes**. Those in the old house may feel insecure in the presence of newer and prettier houses. The chi escapes through the cracks that may mean losses for the people in the house. The difference of the house from its neighbors may also result to disharmony.

- **Landfills and Garbage Piles.** Aside from smelling bad, trash and clutter can cause people to become ill. Energy-wise, garbage and discarded items emit negative chi.

In summary, stay away from areas and objects that cause harmful effects upon your health and emotional stability. Consider the energies that are generated by nearby things, and decide whether you can live with them or not. If you can't relocate, modify your home: repair damages, clear out garbage, and use Feng Shui remedies. Keep yourself healthy to reduce   negative chi.

Elevation

Where your property is positioned along a hill or an inclined land also matters in Feng Shui:

- **At the peak of a high land mass.** A house at the very top of a mountain or hill is vulnerable. There is no protection at its back and sides, thus it is open to all kinds of dangers. It is very visible to wrongdoers. These conditions can make dwellers paranoid.

- **Along a steep hillside.** Aside from being landslide-prone, the chi on a steep incline tends to roll down. As a result, the house won't be able to hold on to chi that comes from the mountain. Finances and good luck will likewise slip away from the inhabitants.

- **Along a gently sloping hill.** This is the best location for a house. It receives support from the hill and it can capture the chi that flows along the land. It is also safe from flooding, which is common among low-lying areas.

- **Flat land.** This may also be favorable for as long as it's not flood-prone. The level terrain offers stable and fortunate chi.

Shape of lots

The shape of the lot affects how energy flows around the building:

- **Square and Rectangle.** These shapes are the best for lots. It's ideal if the house is placed in the center of the lot to allow the chi to circulate well.
- **Trapezoid.** This is not recommended because the chi will have a hard time entering and escaping through the short side.
- **Triangle.** This shape is the most unfavorable of all. Its angles produce sha chi (bad energy) that can cause personality disorders, misfortune, and disorientation.
- **Circle.** Circular lots can cause chi to whirl and become overwhelming.
- **Irregular shape.** Lots with irregular shapes move chi erratically and cause instability.

The ideal lot shapes are square and rectangle. You can fix wrongly-shaped lots by adding garden paths, light posts, and other objects that may be arranged to form a boxy shape around your house.

The House/Building and Interiors

House/Building Shape

- **Square and Rectangle.** These shapes encourage chi to move around without turning into poison arrows.
- **Trapezoid.** Like in the trapezoidal lot, chi may get stuck in this kind of house.
- **Triangle.** Triangular houses, such as those with steeply inclined roofs, contain imbalanced chi.
- **Circle.** Since chi easily moves around in corners, a circular house or a dome ceiling causes energy to swirl violently.
- **Wavy.** A wavy house, or one that has differently-leveled ceilings, makes chi bounce. People who feel this effect can become nauseated.
- **U-shaped.** The house should ideally have a center. A U-shaped house doesn't have one. The center represents the family's unity, and without one, the family members may drift apart.
- **L-shaped.** The L-shaped house is very imbalanced and generates poison arrow

chi from its sharp edges. It also lacks a center.

- **House with atrium at the center.** Without a center, the family may not be unified, and a nagging sense of lack may be present. Missing areas in U-shapes, L-shapes, H-shapes, and cross-shapes can also result to a feeling of incompleteness.
- **H-shaped and Cross-shaped.** These have hollows but they have a center at least. The family may remain cohesive but lack at other areas in life.

As with lots, you can balance out uneven chi in a house by using objects to trace an outline along the house. You can also install a roofed terrace above the hollow part and cover it with a light material such as a glass or screen.

House Size and Dimensions

The ground floor symbolizes the parents or the masters while the upper floors stand for their descendants or subordinates. The bottom floor should be the same size or bigger than the top floor/s to ensure that the structure will be stable, and the children and servants will remain under their command. The size of the house should also be in proportion to the occupants, but if not, the place should be big instead of small. A large residence and few occupants result to Yin energy and a nurturing environment. A small space with many people cultivates Yang energy, which is aggressive. You can balance Yin and Yang energies in the house by using symbols and objects that represent the needed.

Gates and Walls

These form the boundary between the property and the environment, thus it can hold chi within it. Damaged walls and gates can leak chi, and they do not offer enough protection from the weather, violence, robbery, and invasion of privacy. The gates should have even panels: according to Feng Shui, if the left is smaller, the husband might die early, and if the right one is, the wife might. The gate should not open outward to prevent chi from leaving. It should not have spikes that point towards the house to avoid launching poison arrows upon it.

The house should not have a gate that forms a lid over it to avoid resembling a coffin. The wall should not have a window – windows are considered as portals where the chi can leave. Besides, the walls should not offer people a space where they can peek inside your property.

Entrances and Exits

Main Door

The main door can be considered as the mouth of the building or house. Majority of the chi that enters passes through this door. Its size should be only a bit bigger than an average person to allow the chi to enter without getting stuck, and to prevent the chi inside the house from going out. The objects nearby should also be considered, since they will determine the forms of Chi that will enter. Do not place the following things directly in front of the main door:

- Storage room – to avoid stagnant chi
- Mirror and wall near the door – the chi will reflect back out with these
- Poison arrows from poles, pillars, trees, spikes, angles, and roads
- Toilet – bad chi from the toilet will enter the main door
- Stairs – chi from the house will rush out of the door
- The rear door - good chi will enter and leave your house without staying
- The stove – to prevent burning the chi that enters

Do not place a toilet or a sewer pipe directly above the main door to prevent fortune from running out of the house. Remember: water collects both good and bad chi.

The path leading to the main door should not head straight towards it, but instead curve gently or turn at a right angle from it. It's best if the main door is above street level and not below it to give a sense of security. The main entrance should be pleasant to evoke positive emotions to people who enter so they bring good chi into your abode.

Other doors

Doorways should not have exposed beams over them because they press upon the energetic fields of those who pass through. Do not align doors so that the chi won't rush in and out of the house, or otherwise conflict with each other if the doors belong to different rooms or houses.

Ceilings and Roofs

Roofs should not have holes in them to prevent rain from coming in and good chi from rushing out. Avoid installing uneven ceilings because it discourages the smooth flow of chi. Remove or cover up exposed beams – these disrupt the energy in the house and cause illnesses to those who stay underneath them for prolonged periods of time.

Floors

Floors should not have different levels to avoid creating a string of problems among occupants. In Feng Shui, basements are considered as bad luck because it causes a hollow space where there should be support from the ground. The flooring and carpet's design should not be composed of different sizes and shapes – these depict turbulence. Lines on the floor should not be at right angles to the main door, either. Instead, floor lines should run from the entrance and into the house to invite the chi in.

Stairs

Stairs transfer chi from one level of the house to another. It should not lead to the main door to retain sheng chi (good energy). Do not place a toilet in front of a staircase from an upper level to prevent the chi from being flushed down. Do not install stairs at the center or the north of the house – the center is important in uniting the family and the north is believed to be the residence of the gods. Stairs hollow out the portion of the house where they're located; do not place them in important areas.

Living Room and Dining Room

These rooms should be comfortable for the residents and guests. It should not contain forms of negative chi. These rooms are ideally square or rectangle. If the family will regularly spend their time there, it will be helpful if these are located in the house's center. Remove exposed beams from above the dining table to avoid divisiveness among those who use it. The dining table may be round or oval to encourage the circulation of chi. Do not put a toilet overhead the table – the dirty chi will land on it. Do not hang paintings or pictures of ancestors because these emit Yin energy, which is incompatible with the activities in these rooms. Use Yang energy instead.

Kitchen

The kitchen signifies the wealth of the family. The stove should not be seen from the living room because it is equivalent to exposing the family's treasures to outsiders. Do not let the main door lead to the stove. Let the stove rest against a wall to provide support for the family's finances. Do not put it under a window because it is considered as an open space where chi can leak. Do not align the stove with a sink or a washing machine to avoid disharmony caused by the conflicting fire and water elements. Do not put a water closet, tank, or pump behind a stove because doing so makes it hard for the family to hold on to wealth. An exposed beam over the stove and a stove above water pipes produce similar detrimental results.

Bathroom, Toilet and Water Closet

Do not put these on top of the main doors and other areas where people stay. The dirty chi will fall down and contaminate the energies of the places beneath them. They also cause good chi to wash down, and if they're above the doors leading outside of the house, the sheng chi will be flushed away from the house. All the rooms of the house should ideally have floors that are at the same level (if they're on the same floor) except the bathroom. It should be lower than the surrounding areas to keep the water chi in.

Bedroom

The bedroom is supposed to be a steady and restful place. Do not use round shapes and other designs that suggest movement and Yang energy. Do not align a bed with the bedroom door. Do not align the bedroom door with a kitchen door, a bathroom door, or any kind of door. Do not make it lead to a staircase to avoid being hit by bad chi or being drained away of good chi. Do not place your bed in a slanted position to avert imbalanced chi. Put the bed against a wall, and put it away from a window (to avoid incoming chi).

Do not move your bed between a window and a door – this creates sha chi on both sides (remember parallel streets?). Do not place mirrors that reflect the entire bed to avoid tiredness. Remove exposed beams above the bed

– this causes illnesses and conflicts among couples. Do not position a bed under a staircase to avoid being hit by pressure coming from above. Do not position the bed above a stove or below a water closet (fire energy rises and water sinks, affecting the energy of the sleeper).

Keep the bedroom away from the garage to avoid the noise and fumes of vehicles. The ideal position of the bed: at a right angle from the bedroom door (with no part of the bed being hit by the chi coming from the door), far from the window and door, with enough space at its left and right, and with the head of the bed against the wall.

Office

The office should allow you to focus on your work. Put your desk near a wall, with your back towards the wall. Do not align your desk with a door. Do not stick it against the wall where the door is. Do not expose your back against a window or a door. Do not position your desk in an angle from the walls. Do not place your desk between doors and windows. Stay away from exposed beams on the ceiling. To wrap it up, your office should give you an unobstructed view of the entire place, you should have support at your back, and you should stay away from negative chi from openings and harmful objects.

Altar

Like a church and temple, the altar carries Yin energy. Although spiritual energy is a component of Feng Shui, it is sometimes detrimental to the health and wealth of people. Put the altar in a place separate from other rooms. Do not place the altar inside the bedroom – this exaggerates the Yin energy because the bedroom is already Yin. The deities and ancestors might also feel offended when they are worshipped in the same area where lovemaking and marital conflicts transpire. Place a wall behind the altar to support the chi, and do not align it with doors or place it near, above, or below a water closet or stove. Do not put an altar below a staircase to let your prayers rise to heaven and avoid disrespecting the gods.

General Feng Shui Guidelines

Rooms

Consider yin yang balance and elemental interactions when designing rooms. Remove clutter and arrange objects to stimulate and circulate good chi. Furniture should be at the right size for the room that they are in and they should not block people and energy from passing. Sofas, chairs, and benches receive support when placed against a wall. Light up dim areas and open up windows to dissipate negative, stagnant chi.

Outside the house

Choose a good location for your house. If you notice objects or establishments that emanate negative chi, you can shield your property with trees and shrubs or reflect it with a Feng Shui concave mirror. If you have the budget for it, you may renovate your house and lot to follow Feng Shui recommendations.

Conclusion

I hope that you have enjoyed reading this book on Feng Shui. Having lived for many years in Singapore and observed how many locals firmly believe in Feng Shui and having had many discussions with them relating to this I decided to all follow up and start practicing Feng Shui myself. I am now a believer and the design our house closely follows the Feng Shui principals outline above.

You can go beyond these basic guidelines and achieve specific intentions for as long as you can translate them into symbols. For example, if you want a successful marriage, buy décor in pairs and put them in the bedroom. Or, if you want your wealth to grow, put a mirror in front of your stove to symbolically double your wealth. What's important is that you get items that remind you of what you desire and use them along with the principles given in this book.

Good luck, and may wealth, health, and happiness be at your beck and call!

Bonus Content

As a token of our appreciation Grand Reveur Publications would like to give you access to our exclusive bonus content (including free eBooks!).

Exclusive pre-release access to our latest eBooks Free Grand Reveur eBooks during promotional period.

A method ANYONE can use to publish their own book and make passive income.

Visit the following website to receive this bonus content:

https://ignorelimits.leadpages.net/grandreveur publications/

As this is a limited time offer it would be a shame to miss out, I recommend grabbing these bonuses before reading on.